HOUSING LAW AND

QUESTIONS AND SUGGESTED ANSWERS

Written by Steve Norton

LLB, GDL, MA, MRES, LPC

Dedicated to Barbara and Leah

Acknowledgements

I have drawn on a number of sources in compiling general questions and answers for this book. I have drawn on my own general knowledge and examination revision notes as well as housing law texts and exam guides and updates to compile questions for this series of guides that may be useful for those preparing for law and practice exams as well as advice work. I am a member of the Chartered Institute of Legal Executives (CILEX). I work as a practicing lawyer in employment law mainly in a solicitors firm, but also work in a team of lawyers as a volunteer advisor in a South London legal advice centre, where I also advise clients on housing law matters occasionally.

INTRODUCTION

I studied housing law many years ago as an undergraduate and more recently as an elective within the Legal Practice Course (LPC) more recently. I also provide advice to clients attending a legal advice centre in Waterloo as part of the team of volunteer lawyers. I hope that those studying this area of law, and anyone else interested in housing law and practice find the question and answer format useful to grasp the fundamentals of housing law. This format is aimed at the practical application of housing law rather than at any attempt at academic discussion or analysis of housing law, aimed more at those starting legal practice courses. I have used a number of practical questions and suggested answers. I will deal with examination type problem questions and suggested answers in a future volume.

I hope you find these guides useful for your studies, or anyone else who may be interested in learning some of the practical aspects of housing law. This is not a detailed text on all aspects of housing but hopefully it will provide a basic understanding of the key concepts. Organisation like the Legal Action Group provide (LAG) provide excellent comprehensive books on housing law.

I have structured this book in a similar way to others I have written in the series on other areas of law.

CONTENTS

CHAPTER 1

Brief overview of housing law

CHAPTER 2

Overview of types of tenancies in the private rental sector

CHAPTER 3

Overview of types of tenancies in the public rental sector

CHAPTER 4

Repair obligations of landlords and tenants

CHAPTER 5

Grounds of possession

CHAPTER 6

Homelessness

CHAPTER 7

Procedure to be followed by a landlord or mortgagee when seeking possession of premises

CHAPTER 8

How can tenants challenge possession orders

Table of cases

Abbey National Mortgages v Barnard [1996] 71 P & CR 257 CA

Austin v Southwark [2010] 3 WLR 144 UKSC

Akram v Adam [2005] 1 All ER 741, CA

Amicus Horizon Ltd v Mabbott's Estate [2012] EWCA Civ 895

Austin v Southwark [2010] 3 WLR 144 UKSC

Bankway Properties Ltd v Penfold-Dunsford and Leech [2001] 1 WLR 1369, CA

British Anzani (Felixstowe) Ltd v International Marine Management (UK) Ltd [1980] QB 137

Camden LBC v Mallet [2001] 33 HLR, CA

Chelsea Yacht and Boat Co Ltd v Pope [2001] 1 WLR 1941

Clark v Grant [1950] 1 KB 104, CA

Dudley & District Benefit Society v Emerson [1949] Ch 707, CA

Jones v London Borough of Merton [2008] EWCA Civ 660

Knowsley Housing Trust v White [2008] UKHL,70 [2009]

Lambeth LBC v Henry [2000] 32 HLR 874 CA

Lambeth LBC v Howard (2001) 33 HLR 58, CA

Lister v Lane [1893] 2 QB 212, CA

Liverpool City Council v Irwin [1977] AC 239, HL

London and Quadrant Housing Trust v Root [2005] HLR 28, CA

Lurcott v Wakely [1911] 1 KB 905

Manchester City Council v Finn [2002] EWCA Civ 1998

Manel v Memon (2001) 33 HLR 235, CA

McDougall v Easington DC (1989) 21 HLR 310, CA

McAuley v Bristol City Council [1992] 1 QB 134, CA

Table of statutes

ADMINISTRATION OF JUSTICE ACT 1970 & 1973

ANTI-SOCIAL BEHAVIOUR ACT 2003

ANTI-SOCIAL BEHAVIOUR, CRIME AND POLICING ACT 2014

CIVIL PARNERSHIP ACT 2004

CONSUMER CREDIT ACT 1974

COUNTY COURTS ACT 1984

DEFECTIVE PREMISES ACT 1972

DISPLACED PERSONS (TEMPORARY PROTECTION) REGULATIONS 2005 (SI 2005/1379)

FAMILY LAW ACT 1996

HOMELESSNESS REDUCTION ACT 2017

HOUSING AND REGENERATION ACT 2008

HOUSING ACT 1985

HOUSING ACT 1988

HOUSING ACT 1996

LANDLORD AND TENANTS ACT 1927

LANDLORD AND TENANTS ACT 1954

LANDLORD AND TENANTS ACT 1985

LOCALISM ACT 2011

MATRIMONIAL HOMES ACT 1967

MORTGAGE REPOSSESSIONS (PROTECTION OF TENANTS ETC) ACT 2010

OCCUPIERS LIABILITY ACT 1957

PROTECTION FROM EVICTION ACT 1977

PUBLIC ORDER ACT 1986

RENT ACT 1977

RENT (AGRICULTURE) ACT 1976

Statutory Instruments / Regulations

Assured and Protected Tenancies (Lettings to Students) Regulations 1998 (SI 1998/1967)

Displaced Persons (Temporary Protection) Regulations 2005 (SI 2005/1379)

The Flexible Tenancies (Review Procedures) Regulations 2012 (SI 2012/695)

White papers / Bills

White Paper - A Fairer Private Rented Sector on 16 June 2022.

Renters Reform Bill proposed - 2022-23

Chapter 1

Brief overview of housing law

General questions and suggested answers

Question

What is housing law?

Suggested answer

Housing law draws on certain aspects of property law, as well as some elements of public law. From property law, this consists of residential landlord and tenant law (sometimes described as landlord and tenant law). Public law is relevant when you look at the obligations owed to tenants by local authorities and standards in housing in areas they are responsible for. For example:-

- Action needed to be taken against owners who harass residential occupiers;
- Provide housing to certain categories of people

Question

What are the property law aspects of housing law?

Suggested answer

Where residential landlord and tenant law is concerned, housing law is centred around the *contractual rights* between the parties as backed up by relevant statute which has provided greater rights for occupiers. These include:-

- Rights to prevent occupiers from losing their homes;
- Provide security and rent control;
- Provide security of tenure;
- Impose repair obligations.

There are different statutory frameworks with varying degrees of security for residential tenants which originate from the common law contractual landlord and tenant relationship for instance 'private sector' or 'public sector' tenants.

Question

What are the public law aspects of housing law?

Suggested answer

Public law is concerned with the obligations by a local authority often referred to as a local housing authority (LHA) to uphold standards in housing. These would include for instance disrepair and dealing with harassment by owners of tenants which may involve criminal sanctions.

Chapter 2

Overview of types of tenancies in the private rental sector

Question

What are Assured Tenancies?

Suggested answer

Assured Tenancies (AT) were created by the <u>Housing Act 1988</u> (HA 1996). Nearly all new residential tenancies in the private rental sector granted after 15 January 1989 will be AT or Assured Shorthold Tenancies (ASTs), provided they meet certain qualifying conditions. The Housing Act 1996 (HA 1996) amended the HA 1988 to the extent that all tenancies drawn up after February 1997 are ASTs unless stated otherwise.

Under s.1 of the HA 1988 it provides that a tenancy under which a dwelling-house is let as a separate dwelling will be an assured tenancy if and so long as:

(a) The tenant or each joint tenant is an individual; and
(b) The tenant or at least one joint tenant occupies the dwelling as his only or principal home; and
(c) The tenancy is not excluded by Pt I of Sch 1 to the HA 1988 from becoming an assured
tenancy.

Question

What is meant by let as a separate dwelling?

Suggested answer

The property must be let as a *dwelling house.* The HA 1988 s.45 states a dwelling house can be a house or a part of a house. This would include a flat or a house. In *Uratemp Ventures Ltd v Collins* [2002] 1 AC 301 HL a room in a hotel was found to meet the requirement of a dwelling house (with or without cooking facilities which were not considered crucial). The tenant must have exclusive use of some accommodation. Living accommodation can include a living room, bedroom and kitchen, but not a bathroom or toilet. In the case of joint tenants they are regarded as a single entity so can share. A person has exclusive occupation of any accommodation, for instance his/her bedroom but in addition under the terms of his/her tenancy agreement shares living accommodation such as a living room and kitchen with others (as long as none are the landlord). In these circumstances s.3 HA 1988 provides that the separate accommodation will be seen as a dwelling-house let on an Assured Tenancy. However, the dwelling must form part of the land or will not qualify as a separate dwelling if it is not part of the land. In *Chelsea Yacht and Boat Co Ltd v Pope* [2001] 1 WLR 1941, CA a houseboat although gas, electricity, water, phone and sewage services were connected, will not count as a dwelling house.

Question

What is meant by only or principal home?

Suggested answer

The tenant must occupy the dwelling-house as his only or principal home to be an assured tenant. This means there must be outward signs that the house can be occupied as a home such as furniture or personal effects. There must also be an intention by the tenant where he is not physically living there, to come back to the home.

Where the dwelling-house formed the matrimonial home and the spouse or civil partner who is the sole tenant, leaves the property, the non-tenant spouse or civil partner who remains in occupation is deemed to occupy on behalf of the absent tenant while the marriage or civil partnership lasts. This is covered under the s.30 of the Family Law Act 1996, as amended by the Civil Partnership Act 2004.

Question

Are there categories of tenancies excluded from Assured Tenancy Status?

Suggested answer

There are a number of tenancies that even where they meet the definitions in s.1 cannot be Assured (Schedule 1). These are:-

(a) Subject to certain exceptions, tenancies entered into before, or pursuant to a contract made before, the HA 1988 came into effect on 15 January 1989;
(b) High-value premises, i.e. where the rateable value for pre-1 April 1990 lettings exceeded £1,500 in Greater London or £750 elsewhere; or where a letting on or after 1 April 1990 has an annual rent exceeding £25,000 in Wales and, from 1 October 2010, £100,000 in England;
(c) Tenancies at no or low rent, ie where no rent is payable or where for pre-1 April 1990 lettings the rent was less than two-thirds the rateable value of the dwelling-house on 31 March 1990; or for lettings on or after 1 April 1990, the rent payable in Greater London is £1,000 or less a year, or £250 or less a year elsewhere.

CASE EXAMPLE

In *Ujima HA v Ansah* (1997) 30 HLR 831, CA, the defendant, had an Assured Tenancy from the claimant and let out the flat on an Assured Shorthold Tenancy. The claimant sought possession of the flat on the basis that the defendant had lost his assured tenant status. The defendant argued that he had left furniture in the flat and intended to return. It was held that the matter had to be looked at objectively. On that basis, the defendant showed no outward signs of the property remaining his principal home as he had left no personal belongings in it. The furniture, left by the defendant in the flat, could be construed as being consistent with the sub-letting, particularly since the defendant was able to obtain almost four times the amount of rent from the sub-tenant as that which he had to pay for his Assured Tenancy. It was also clear that the defendant could not easily regain occupation of the property while the sub-tenancy was in existence.

(d) Business tenancies to which Pt II of the Landlord and Tenant Act (LTA) 1954 applies;
(e) Licensed premises for the sale and consumption of intoxicating liquors;
(f) Tenancies of agricultural land where agricultural land (as defined in s 26(3)(a) General Rates Act 1967), exceeding two acres, is let together with the dwelling-house;
(g) Tenancies of agricultural holdings where the dwelling-house is comprised in an agricultural holding (within the meaning of the Agricultural Holdings Act 1986) or farm business and is occupied by the person responsible for control of the farming or management of the holding;
(h) Lettings to students who are pursuing or intend to pursue a course of studies and where the letting is provided by a specified educational institution. The institutions specified are universities and colleges listed in the Assured and Protected Tenancies (Lettings to Students) Regulations 1998 (SI 1998/1967) as amended;
(i) Holiday letting, where this is the purpose of the letting;
(j) Resident landlords;
(k) Lettings by public bodies, ie the Crown, local authorities etc;
(l) A tenancy provided by a private landlord for asylum-seekers under Pt VI of the Immigration and Asylum Act 1999;
(m) A tenancy provided by a private landlord for persons with temporary protection under the Displaced Persons (Temporary Protection) Regulations 2005 (SI 2005/1379);

(n) A family intervention tenancy granted by a registered provider of social housing or an RSL who has complied with the requirements in para 12ZA of Sch 1; and
(o) A protected tenancy under the Rent Act1977 (RA 1977); a housing association tenancy within Pt VI of the RA 1977; a secure tenancy; and a protected occupier within the Rent (Agriculture) Act 1976. [i]

Question

What sort of terms are found in Assured Tenancies?

Suggested answer

The Landlord and Tenant will agree terms (basically the Landlord sets the terms). There is little in the way of statutory intervention. There are however, certain implied terms found in the HA 1988 such as ss.13 to 18 relating to rent increases, assignment of an succession for periodic assured tenancies as well as a right of access to carry out repairs, and a right under statute for lawful assured sub-tenants' tenancies to continue after termination of their landlord's interest in the property.

Question

How are rents increased for periodic assured tenants?

Suggested answer

Landlord's in the private rented sector can charge a 'market rent'. Assured tenants of Registered Social Landlords (RSLs) and Registered Providers of Social Housing (PRPs) are in a slightly better position with rents slightly below the private sector. In the case of tenancy agreements with RSLs normally have an express term that covers with the way in which rent will be increased. This term where it is included must ensure that the correct procedure for increases in the rent is followed otherwise it may not be due lawfully.

A landlord may include a rent review clause determining when rent will be increased. If this is not the case, in an Assured Periodic Tenancy, then by s.13 of the HA 1988, for him/her to increase the rent, he/she needs to serve a prescribed notice to commence a procedure to increase the rent. If the tenant feels the rent suggested by the landlord is excessive and well above the current market rents in that area, he/she can refer to a Rent Assessment Committee which has the power to determine a market rent for the property under s.14 HA 1988. It is important to stress that the parties are free to vary the rental terms by agreement without resorting to the notice procedures (s.13(5)). If a Rent Assessment Committee determines an open rent in excess of £100,000 per year, the tenancy will then no longer be an Assured Tenancy (*R v London Rent Assessment Panel, ex p Cadogan Estates* [1998] QB 398).

Thus in reality rent control does not exist for assured tenants unless a rent increase can be challenged as fictitious or repugnant - *Bankway Properties Ltd v Penfold-Dunsford and Leech* [2001] 1 WLR 1369, CA).

Question

Are there terms in the HA 1988 dealing with assignment and sub-letting for Periodic Assured Tenants?

Suggested answer

Where there is no express term in the Periodic Assured Tenancy agreement that covers the tenant's right to assign or sub-let, then s.15 of the HA 1988 implies into the agreement a term that the tenant cannot assign or sub-let without the landlord's consent. It is important to note that the landlord is not required to be reasonable in refusing his/her consent. Section 15 HA 1988 has the effect of overriding the general provision found in s.19 of the Landlord and Tenant Act 1927 (LTA 1927) which usually requires the landlord to be reasonable in exercising his/her discretion. This will apply to all periodic tenancies which do not contain an express term and all statutory periodic tenancies (with or without express terms in the original fixed-term agreement).

Question

What are the succession rights for periodic assured tenancies?

Suggested answer

By S.17 of the HA 1988, the spouse or civil partner of a sole tenant to an Assured Periodic Tenancy, can succeed to an Assured Tenancy. The only condition to be satisfied is that the spouse or civil partner was occupying the dwelling-house as his or her only or principal home immediately before the tenant's death. Where a person was living with the tenant as his or her spouse or civil partner they are also eligible to succeed under S. 7(4)). It should be noted that the requirement that the successor must have been 'living with' the deceased is fairly strictly construed by the courts. Two useful cases:-

CASE EXAMPLE -

In *Amicus Horizon Ltd v Mabbott's Estate* [2012] EWCA Civ 895 the defendant was unable to show that he was entitled to succeed to a tenancy. He relied on S.17(4) HA 1988. He had been living with his partner before she died in her flat, for 10 years. Although they had had a close loving relationship, his partner had been keen to retain her own independence and not be seen as in a husband and wife or similar relationship. Another factor was that they claimed benefits separately. This did not amount to an open and unequivocal display to the outside world.

However in another case a different decision was reached:-

CASE EXAMPLE -

In *Nutting v Southern Housing Group Ltd* [2004] EWHC 2982 (Ch), it was held that to be treated as a spouse the relationship had to be an emotional one that involves a lifetime of commitment, rather than one of convenience, friendship, companionship or the living together of lovers. The relationship must be openly and unequivocally displayed to the outside world.

The right of succession will not be available where the deceased person was himself a successor tenant. (S.17(1D)). The term `successor tenant' is widely defined by the courts and will include:-

- (a) where the deceased succeeded under S.17;
- (b) (b) where he was originally one of two or more joint tenants of the property and became the sole tenant by survivorship;
- (c) where the deceased gained the tenancy under the will or intestacy of a previous tenant;

(d) where he was a successor to the Assured Tenancy as a result of the RA 1977 succession;

It is important to note that these succession provisions do not apply to fixed-term assured tenancies. Where a fixed-term tenant dies , the normal rules will apply with the tenancy passing under the deceased tenant's will or intestacy. Similarly, this will also be the situation in an Assured Periodic Tenancy where there is no one eligible to succeed under the s 17 provisions. However, as the 2015 CLP guide makes clear in this instance, the landlord will have a mandatory ground for possession[ii].

<u>Succession rights for periodic or fixed-term assured tenants of PRP landlords.</u>

S.17 of the HA 1988 (as amended) can enable succession rights on the death of a sole tenant. This right of succession can occur in certain circumstances:-

- ❖ a periodic tenancy of a fixed-term tenancy of not less that two years;
- ❖ granted by a PRP landlord in England on on before 1 April 2012.

The successor can be:-

- ❖ a spouse or civil partner occupying the dwelling as his or her only or principal home; or

❖ a person who was living with the tenant as a spouse or civil partner

Another situation could be where there is not a spouse or civil partner, succession can go to a person who meets the terms of the tenancy agreement.

It should also be noted that for tenancies created before 1 April 2012 and to non-PRP landlords who grant Assured Tenancies after that date, the previous unamended provisions of the S.17 HA 1988 still apply.

28

Chapter 3

Overview of types of tenancies in the public rental sector

Question

What are the different types of tenancies offered by local authorities/social landlords?

Suggested answer

A summary of the types of tenancies –

- o Secure tenancies (generally periodic tenancies for life;
- o Flexible fixed term tenancies under Localism Act 2011;
- o Introductory tenancies;
- o Demoted tenancies.

Question

What are Secure Tenancies?

Suggested answer

Most council tenants are secure tenants.
A secure tenancy is a lifetime tenancy. A tenant who is allocated accommodation by an LHA or Housing Action Trust (HAT) may be a secure tenant. Where a tenancy or licence where it involves a dwelling-house let as a separate dwelling (covered in an earlier question), is a secure tenancy at any time when the

landlord condition and the tenant condition is met (S.79 HA 1985). The letting may be for a fixed-term or may be periodic.

The Localism Act 2012 gave LHAs the option of granting a new form of tenancy called the 'flexible tenancy' (new provision introduced to the HA 1985 – ss 107A-107E).

Question

What is the Landlord condition?

Suggested answer

Under the Landlord condition the landlord can be:-

- ✓ a local authority;
- ✓ a new town corporation;
- ✓ a HAT;
- ✓ an urban development corporation (S.80 HA 1985);
- ✓ a Mayoral development corporation; or
- ✓ in certain situations, Homes England / Regulator of Social Housing (previously work performed by the Homes and Communities Agency (HCA), the Greater London Authority or the Welsh minister.

Secure tenancies were introduced by the HA 1980. Before the HA 1988 tenancies enjoyed secure tenant status along with RSLs and PRPs until 15 January 1989 (when this Act came into effect). Any new tenants of RSLs and PRPs will not be secure tenants from this point.

Question

What is the tenant condition?

Suggested answer

The tenant condition means a tenant must be an individual who occupies the dwelling-house as his only or principal home (s.81 HA 1985). If there is a joint tenancy then each of the joint tenants must be an individual and at least one of them must occupy the dwelling-house as his only or principal home.

Question

What are Flexible Fixed-Term Tenancies?

Suggested answer

The Localism Act 2011 introduced a power for local authorities to offer 'Flexible Tenancies' to new social tenants after 1 April 2012. Flexible Tenancies are secure fixed-term tenancies with a minimum term of two years. The 2011 Act also allowed housing associations to offer fixed-term tenancies to all new tenants after 1 April 2012.

LHAs now have a power to grant flexible tenancies under s.107A of the HA 1985 instead of or in addition to the normal periodic secure tenancies.
Under s.107A(2), a flexible tenancy is a secure tenancy if:
(a) it is granted by an LHA (or other landlord within s. 80 HA of the 1985) in England for a term certain of not less than two years; and
(b) before it was granted, the person who became the landlord under the tenancy served a written notice on the person who became the tenant under the tenancy stating that the tenancy would be a Flexible Tenancy. Written notice that a Flexible Tenancy will be created can be served on:
(a) new tenants of the LHA;
(b) an introductory tenant notifying him, prior to the start of the introductory tenancy, that at the end of the introductory period he will become a secure flexible tenant;
(c) a family intervention tenant who was previously a secure flexible tenant ; and
(d) a demoted tenant who was previously a secure flexible tenant

Review of a flexible tenancy

The person served with a written notice has 21 days, or such longer time as the LHA agrees, to request a review of the decision. However, the only basis of challenge is that the length of the term does not accord with a policy of the prospective landlord as to the length of the terms of the flexible tenancies it grants (s 107B).

The Flexible Tenancies (Review Procedures) Regulations 2012 (SI 2012/695) set out the procedure for such reviews. This gives the applicant a right to request an oral hearing. [iii]

Question

What are Introductory Tenancies?

Suggested answer

Introductory tenancies were created by the Housing Act 1996.

An introductory tenancy is a probationary or trial tenancy granted to a new tenant that allows the local authority landlord or Housing Action Trust (HAT) to decide if they are a suitable tenant. They were intended to give local authorities more power to deal with anti-social behaviour. In practice, however, they have had a much wider application, for example as a way of dealing with rent arrears.

Local authorities and HATs can elect to have an introductory tenancy scheme. They can revoke the scheme at any time.[iv]

Question

What are Demoted Tenancies?

Suggested answer

A demoted tenancy is a form of tenancy that reduces a tenant's security of tenure and rights for 12 to 18 months (ss.14 and 15, and Sch.1 Anti-social Behaviour Act 2003). Demoted tenancies were brought in by the Housing Act 1996, giving social landlords the power to apply to demote secure or assured tenancies in cases of anti-social behaviour.

There are two types of demoted tenancy - Local authority (or HAT) secure or flexible tenancies are demoted to demoted tenancies. If the Court approves that application, then the security of tenure for that tenancy falls away for 12 months.

The council must show that you have:-

- Behaved anti-socially in the area or to council staff

- Used your home for illegal activities such as drug dealing

The council must give you:-

- At least 4 weeks' notice in writing on a special form

- Reasons why it's applying for a demotion order

The council have 12 months from when the notice expires to apply to the court to demote your tenancy.

Chapter 4

Repair obligations of landlords and tenants

Question

Where are the general repair obligations found?

Suggested answer

Section 11 of the Landlord and Tenant Act 1985 sets out the repair obligations of the landlord and tenant. These cannot be excluded by any informal agreement between the landlord and tenant.

Question

What are the Landlord's repair obligations in Section 11?

Suggested answer

Section 11(1) of the LTA 1985 implies into certain tenancies granted after 23 October 1961 a contractual obligation on the landlord:-

(a) to keep in repair the structure and exterior of the dwelling-house (including drains, gutters and external pipes);

(b) to keep in repair and proper working order the installations in the dwelling-house for the supply of water, gas, electricity and for sanitation (including basins, sinks, baths and sanitary conveniences, but not other fixtures, fittings and appliances for making use of the supply of water, gas or electricity); and

(c) to keep in repair and proper working order the installations in the dwelling-house for
space heating and heating water.

Question

Where are the contractual repair obligations found?

Suggested answer

There may be repair obligations in the tenancy agreement in the form of express terms. There may be implied terms also. It is an implied term that the premises will be fit for human habitation at the start of the tenancy (*Smith v Marrable* (1843) 11 M & W 5). In *Liverpool City Council v Irwin* [1977] AC 239, HL, the tenancy agreement imposed no obligation on the landlords to keep the common parts of a large block of flats, such as lifts, stair lighting and rubbish chutes, in repair. As the tenants needed to use these common parts, it was necessary to imply a contractual obligation on the landlord to take reasonable care to maintain those common parts in a state of reasonable repair.

The tenant has an implied obligation to use the premises in a tenant-like manner (see *Warren v Keen* [1954] 1 QB 15). This could include doing small jobs such as keeping windows clean, unblocking sinks, changing lightbulbs etc. If there is an implied right at common law for the landlord to carry out repairs, there will be a corresponding obligation on the tenant to allow the landlord access to put those repairs into effect (*McAuley v Bristol City Council* [1992] 1 QB 134, CA).

Question

What is the Tenant's obligation on repairs?

Suggested answer

Lord Esher MR discussed the tenant's covenant to repair in *Lister v Lane* [1893] 2 QB 212, CA:-

'a covenant to repair a house is not a covenant to give a different thing from that which the tenant took when he entered into the covenant. He has to repair that thing which he took; he is not obliged to make a new and different thing ...'

Repair can include replacement or renewal of a part of the house (*Lurcott v Wakely* [1911] 1 KB 905) but not rebuilding a house which has fallen down, only the part which is in need of repair. To keep an old house in good condition is likely to require more work in terms of repair than that expected to keep a new house in good condition (*Proudfoot v Hart* [1890] 25 QBD 42, CA).

Question

Is there a difference between 'repair' and 'improvement'?

Suggested answer

In *Ravenseft Properties Ltd v Davstone Holdings Ltd* [1980] QB 12, it was held that repairs could include improvement. New cladding incorporated new expansion joints to prevent stone cladding falling off the walls, and it was held the work was capable of amounting to repair.

In *McDougall v Easington DC* (1989) 21 HLR 310, CA, the test to determine what constitutes a repair of improvement was discussed. Mustill LJ looked at earlier cases that considered what may amount to a repair or improvement. Based upon the nature and age of the premises, their condition when the tenant o started to occupy, and the other express terms of the tenancy: He discussed three different tests:-

(i) whether the alterations went to the whole or substantially the whole of the structure or to only a subsidiary part;

(ii) whether the effect of the alterations was to produce a building of a wholly different character from that which had been let;
(iii) what was the cost of the works in relation to the previous value of the building, and what was their effect on the value and lifespan of the building.

The act of putting in a damp-proof course where none had existed before in an old building, did not amount to repair (*Wainwright v Leeds City Council* (1984) 270 EG 1289.

Question

What if the obligation to repair premises is on the Landlord?

Suggested answer

Where the obligation to repair premises let to the tenant is on the landlord, the obligation will not arise until the landlord has *notice of the defect*, whether from the tenant or otherwise, expressed or implied (*O'Brien v Robinson* [1973] AC 912, HL). Express terms are likely to be found in the tenancy agreement that impose obligations on the landlord, but they must not seek to reduce or negate the repairing obligations imposed on the landlord by statute (LTA 1985, S.12).

Question

Are there other statutory repair obligations that may arise for the Landlord?

Suggested answer

The Occupiers' Liability Act 1957 (OLA 1957) may apply where the landlord retains possession of, and therefore control over, parts of a building, such as the common parts of a block of flats. Where the state of repair of those parts results in the tenant, or other person being injured, the landlord may be liable. Under S.2 of the OLA 1957, the landlord has a common law duty to take such care as in all the circumstances of the case is reasonable, to see that the visitor will be reasonably safe when using the premises for the purposes for which he is permitted to be there.

The Defective Premises Act 1972 (S.4) imposes a duty of care on landlords in two circumstances –

1. The first duty comes about because of the landlords' repairing obligation.
2. The second duty may arise as a consequence of a right the landlord may have to carry out maintenance or repairs.

Question

What are some examples of remedies open to a Tenant for the Landlord's breach of his/her repair obligations?

Suggested answer

Examples of remedies available will differ for public and private rental tenants but they some of the main remedies could be:-

- **Self-help** – set off (set off the costs of repairs against future rent payments)
- **Specific performance** (the court may make an order of specific performance against a landlord in breach of his obligation to keep in repair a dwelling, or any part of the premises in which the dwelling is comprised (s.17 of the LTA 1985)
- **Damages** (i.e. breach of the express or implied covenant to repair)
- **Injunction** (an interim injunction may be applied for in exceptional circumstances, but the court must be satisfied that there is an immediate need for the work to be done such as a real risk to health)
- **Complaint to an ombudsman** (the tenant can complain to the Housing Ombudsman where it can be shown failure to repair amounts to maladministration, which can be argued to be causing, or has caused, injustice – he/she has the power to investigate and make recommendations or determinations.

Question

What are some examples of remedies open to a Landlord's for the Tenant's breach of his/her repair obligations?

Suggested answer

Examples of the general remedies available for landlords could be:-

- **Self-help** (Where there is a right, either in the lease or by statute, to enter and do repair works that the tenant ought to have done)
- **Damages** (Landlord can recover damages for the lower of the cost of repair or diminished value of the premises
- **Forfeiture/possession proceedings** (Forfeiture will bring the lease to an end with a view to regaining possession of the premises with no compensation payable to tenants.
- **Specific performance** (May be available to a landlord against a tenant in disrepair, in some rare circumstances (*Rainbow Estates v Tokenhold* [1998] 2 All ER 860)

46

Chapter 5

Grounds of possession

Question

How do the courts decide upon granting possession orders?

Suggested answer

Under the HA 1988 (s.5) a periodic assured tenancy can only be brought to an end by an order of the court. The court must be satisfied that that one or more of the grounds set out in the HA 1988 (s.7), Schedule 2 is shown before an order of possession can be issued. The court will have no discretion where one of the mandatory grounds under s.2 are made out (HA 1988, Schedule 2, Part I), the court has no discretion and must make an order for possession, subject to HA 1988, s.7(5A) and s.7(6). If the courts is satisfied that any of the discretionary grounds are made out subject to HA 1988, s.7(5A) and s.7(6), they may make an order for possession, or not depending on how they decide to apply their discretion.

Question

What are the grounds of possession?

Suggested answer

Grounds 1 to 8 are mandatory grounds for possession:

- Ground 1 – Recovery by owner or future occupier
- Ground 2 – Mortgagees
- Ground 3 – Out-of-season holiday lets
- Ground 4 – Recovery of student accommodation
- Ground 5 – Ministers of religion
- Ground 6 – Recovery for redevelopment
- Ground 7 – Death of the tenant
- Ground 7A – Anti-social behaviour
- Ground 7B – Right to rent
- Ground 8 – Eight weeks' or 2 months' worth or rent arrears

Grounds 9 to 17 are discretionary grounds for possession:

- Ground 9 – Suitable alternative accommodation
- Ground 10 – Rent arrears
- Ground 11 – Persistent delays in paying rent
- Ground 12 – Breach of any obligation
- Ground 13 – Waste or neglect
- Ground 14 – Nuisance/annoyance or criminal conviction
- Ground 14A – Violence to occupier
- Ground 15 – Deterioration of furniture
- Ground 16 – Premises let to employees
- Ground 17 – Tenancy induced by false statement

Grounds 1 to 8 are mandatory grounds for possession

Question

When does Ground 1 apply?

Suggested answer

Ground 1 – Recovery by owner occupier or future occupier

There are two situations where this ground will apply
> (a) Where an owner occupier wants to let out his property; and
> (b) Where an owner buys a property with the intention to reside in it at some future date but wishes to let it out in the meantime.

In either of the above situations the owner should have given notice at the start of the tenancy to the assured tenant, that they could be pursued for possession on this ground. It is the case that the court does have discretion to dispense with the notice if it considers it just and equitable (*Mustafa v Ruddock* [1998] 30 HLR 495, CA). In cases where the landlord is a joint owner then one of them can apply for possession under this ground.

In the case of category (a) it should be said that at least one of the joints the landlords must have occupied the dwelling as his only or principal home at some point before it was let out. Under category (b), the landlord, or at least one joint landlord, must show that he requires possession of the property for occupation as his or his spouse's or civil partner's only or principal home. In the case of ground (b) it does not apply to a landlord who bought the property after the assured tenancy was created (i.e. bought the reversion). Also, where landlords are 'legal persons' such as RSLs and PRPs this ground could not be used.

Question

When does Ground 2 apply?

Suggested answer

Ground 2 – recovery by mortgagees

Ground 2 will apply where a property is subject to a mortgage which existed before the Assured Tenancy was granted and the mortgagor has not kept up with the mortgage payments. This ground will entitle a mortgagee to obtain possession for the purpose of sale with vacant possession, provided the tenant had written notice before the tenancy was created or the court decides that it is just and equitable to dispense with notice. If the landlord has granted the Assured Tenancy without the consent of the mortgagee and in breach of the terms of the mortgage, then the mortgagee will be able to, as the illegal tenancy will not be binding on the mortgagee (*Dudley & District Benefit Society v Emerson* [1949] Ch 707, CA).

Question

When does Ground 3 apply?

Suggested answer

Ground 3 – Out-of-season holiday lets

This ground allows premises that would otherwise be used for holiday lettings to be let out on Assured Tenancies, presumably out of season. However, in order for this ground to apply the landlord must have given written notice to the tenant before the start of the tenancy and the dwelling house must have been occupied under a holiday letting within the period of 12 months before the start of the Assured Tenancy.

Question

When does Ground 4 apply?

Suggested answer

Ground 4 – Recovery of student accommodation

This ground enables specified education institutions that are listed in the Assured and Protected Tenancies (Lettings to Students) Regulations 1998 (SI 1998/1967) as amended) to recover possession of premises which were let out on an Assured Tenancy for a fixed term not exceeding 12 months. The landlord will have needed to have served notice at the beginning of the tenancy that possession could be recovered on this ground, and the premises had been let out as a student let within Sch 1 to the HA 1988 within the preceding 12 months.

Question

When does Ground 5 apply?

Suggested answer

Ground 5 – Recovery of premises for a minister of religion

This ground is satisfied where the landlord has given written notice at the beginning of the Assured Tenancy, that the dwelling-house is held for the purpose of being available for occupation by a minister of religion as a residence from which to perform his duties. If the court is satisfied that possession is required for this purpose, then the landlord can obtain possession under this ground.

Question

When does Ground 6 apply?

Suggested answer

Ground 6 – Recovery for redevelopment

Where a landlord did not acquire his interest for money or money's worth after the tenancy was created, wishes to demolish, reconstruct or carry out substantial works to the whole of a substantial part of the dwelling-house and is unable to do this without obtaining possession, this ground will apply.
Where an Assured Tenancy arose as a result as a result of the Rent At 1977 this will not apply.
In these circumstances the landlord must establish that possession is necessary and that he is ready to proceed with the redevelopment.

The tenant will be entitled to his reasonable removal expenses if possession is obtained under this ground (HA 1988, s.11).

Question

When does Ground 7 apply?

Suggested answer

Ground 7 – Death of the tenant

Where an assured periodic tenant, a statutory periodic tenant, or a fixed term tenant in England dies and his tenancy passes under his will or on intestacy the landlord will be able to obtain possession against the new tenant provided he commences proceedings within 12 months of the date of death, or within 12 months of becoming aware of the death (as determined by the court). In this case proceedings commence with the issue of a court claim, not the s.8 notice (see *Shepping v Osada* (2001) 33 HLR 146, CA).

It should be noted that accepting rent from the new tenant will not be regarded as creating a new tenancy, unless the landlord has agreed in writing to changes in the terms of the tenancy.

Question

When does Ground 7A apply?

Suggested answer

Ground 7A – Anti-social behaviour

Where any one of the five conditions below relating to anti-social behaviour are met, the court must award possession if the landlord has served a notice of seeking possession.

There are also three discretionary grounds for reasons of antisocial behaviour.

Ground 7A is referred to as an 'absolute ground for possession'. Government guidance on Anti-social Behaviour, Crime and Policing Act 2014 includes a chapter on using this ground.

The required minimum notice length for ground 7A is:

- one month if the tenancy is for a fixed term

- 4 weeks if the tenancy is periodic

Condition 1: Conviction of serious offence

The tenant, or anyone living in or visiting the property, has been convicted of a serious offence that was committed on or after 20 October 2014:

- in the locality of the dwelling house, or

- elsewhere against either a person who lives, or has a right to occupy accommodation, in the locality, or

- elsewhere against the landlord or someone employed (whether or not by the landlord) in connection with the landlord's housing management functions

A serious offence for this purpose must be one of the specific offences set out in Schedule 2A of the Housing Act 1985.

Condition 2: Breach of IPNA

A court found that the tenant, or anyone living in or visiting the property, had breached a provision of an Injunction to Prevent Nuisance or Annoyance (IPNA).

The breach must have occurred in the locality, or elsewhere if the IPNA was granted in order to prevent harassment, alarm or distress to:

- a person who lives, or has a right to occupy accommodation, in the locality

- the landlord or someone employed (whether or not by the landlord) in connection with the landlord's housing management functions

The condition is not met where the breach of the IPNA only relates to a failure to participate in a particular activity.

Condition 2 was not available until 23 March 2015 when Part 1 of the Anti-social Behaviour, Crime and Policing Act 2014 came into effect.

Condition 3: Breach of a Criminal Behaviour Order

The tenant, or anyone living in or visiting the property, has been convicted of a breach of a Criminal Behaviour Order (CBD)that prohibits an activity in the locality, or elsewhere when the CBD was intended to protect:

- a person who lives, or has a right to occupy accommodation, in the locality

- the landlord or someone employed (whether or not by the landlord) in connection with the landlord's housing management functions

Condition 4: Closure order

A Closure Order has been made on the tenant's property and access to the property under the order (and/or a closure notice) has been prohibited for more than 48 hours.

Condition 5: Noise nuisance

The tenant, or anyone living in or visiting the property, has been convicted of an offence under section 80(4) or 82(8) of the Environmental Protection Act 1990 as a result of breaching an abatement notice or court order in relation to noise nuisance committed on or after 20 October 2014.

Condition not met

Conditions 1 to 5 will not be met if an appeal against the conviction, order, or finding is:

- pending

- successful.

Question

When does Ground 7B apply?

Suggested answer

Ground 7B – Right to rent

Section 41 inserted a new mandatory ground (Ground 7B) into the Housing Act 1988 which can be used by landlords where some or all occupiers have no right to rent. As a result, a new prescribed form of Section 8 Notice of Seeking Possession came into force on

1st December 2016 which was amended to include reference to the new mandatory Ground 7B.

Question

When does Ground 8 apply?

Suggested answer

Ground 8 – Recovery for serious arrears

The landlord will be able to recover possession against an assured tenant who pays rent weekly or monthly, if he is able to show the court that, both at the date of the service of a s.8 notice and the date of the hearing, at least eight weeks' rent is unpaid. In the case of a tenancy where the rent is paid monthly, at least two months' rent must be unpaid. A tenancy where rent is paid on a quarterly basis, at least one quarter's rent must be more than three months in arrears. Any rent due must satisfy provision s.48 of the LTA 1987 that rent due will not be treated as lawfully due from the tenant of a dwelling-house unless the landlord has provided the tenant with details of a name and address where notices can be served. Ground 8 is one of three grounds for possession based on rent arrears that are available to landlord of an assured tenant (the other two being discretionary grounds). Ground eight is a mandatory provision and like the other mandatory grounds, must be strictly applied by the court. In *Mountain v Hastings [1995]* 25 HLR 427 CA, a possession order was granted based on Ground 8 arrears, but set aside as the s.8 notice was held to be invalid as it did not include sufficient particulars to the tenant. The discretion in s.8(2) that allowed the landlord to add or alter the notice applied only to a valid notice, in this case as the notice was not valid, this was not applicable. A tenant cannot use a delay in receiving housing benefit as a defence to a s.8 notice nor allow an adjournment of the hearing, to enable housing benefit to be paid to lower the amount of the arrears for the ground to apply (court does not have the discretion to adjourn or suspend in mandatory cases – HA 1988, s.9(6)). But the tenant may have a valid counter-claim against the landlord, and then an adjournment may be possible. An example –

A tenant has a counter-claim for disrepair. The amount of compensation that is likely to be awarded on the counter-claim may be used to cancel out the arrears or bring it down below the limit of the mandatory ground. In this situation, an adjournment to the possession proceedings could be obtained. It can be argued under s.9(6) the court would not be satisfied under this provision that the landlord was entitled to possession under Ground 8 until the counter-claim had been tried (*North British Housing Association Ltd v Matthews* [2005] 2 All ER 667, CA)

Parts II and III – The discretionary grounds for possession

The court has the extended discretion under s.9 of the HA 1988, under the discretionary grounds, to adjourn the proceedings, or to stay, postpone or suspend any possession order made by the court.

Question

When does Ground 9 come into play?

Suggested answer

Ground 9 - Availability of suitable alternative accommodation

Under Ground 9 the court may order possession if the landlord can show that alternative accommodation is available for the Tenant, or will be available when the possession order itself takes effect.

When the court is happy that the accommodation is suitable, they must then decide whether it is reasonable to then make an order for possession under Ground 9.

When does Ground 10 apply?

Suggested answer

Ground 10 – Recovery for rent arrears

To establish this ground for possession the landlord will have to show that at the date of issue of proceedings and also at the date of the service of the S.8 notice, the tenant was in arrears with rent that is lawfully due. If the court decides to dispense with the need for notice under S.8(1)(b), then the only condition that needs to be met is that there were arrears outstanding at the point of the issue of proceedings.

Question

What is Ground 11?

Suggested answer

Ground 11 – Recovery for persistent delay in paying rent

This ground will be satisfied where the tenant persistently delays paying rent that is lawfully due. Even if the tenant is not in arrears at the start of the possession proceedings, the landlord will have satisfied this ground.

Question

When does Ground 12 apply?

Suggested answer

Ground 12 – Recovery for breach of obligation

This ground deals with a situation where the tenant has breached an express or implied obligation of the tenancy agreement. It is worth noting that the court is not likely to exercise its discretion to make a possession order if the breach is not serious. Also, as in *Clark v Grant [1950]* 1 KB 104, CA, the court will not exercise its discretion where the lease can be forfeited, but the landlord has waived the breach by accepting rent, even though aware of the breach.

Question

How does Ground 13 operate?

Suggested answer

Ground 13 – Recovery due to deterioration of the dwelling-house or any of the common parts

This ground may be used where the landlord has shown that the condition of the dwelling-house, or any of the common parts, has deteriorated due to acts of the tenant or any other person (i.e. lodger) residing in the dwelling-house creating waste, or neglect or default. If this is established by the landlord, then this ground will be satisfied. Thus, if a lodger or sub-tenant has committed acts of waste, neglect or default, the tenant is required to take reasonable steps to remove that person, if not, the landlord can rely on this inaction for this ground.

Question

What is Ground 14?

Suggested answer

Ground 14 - Recovery for nuisance, annoyance or criminal activity

This ground can be used by the landlord in situations where the tenant:-

- Has been guilty of conduct causing or likely to cause a nuisance or annoyance to a person residing, visiting or otherwise engaging in a lawful activity in the locality;
- Has been guilty of conduct causing or likely to cause a nuisance or annoyance to the landlord of the dwelling-house, or a person employed (whether or not by the landlord) in connection with the exercise of the landlord's housing management functions, and that is directly or indirectly related to or affects those functions, or;

- Has been convicted for using the premises, or allowing them to be used, for illegal or immoral purposes

- Has been convicted of an indictable offence committed in the locality.

Ground 14A – Domestic violence

This ground only applies to assured tenancies granted by private registered providers of social housing or charitable housing trusts. It can be used where the property has been occupied by a married couple, a couple who have entered into a civil partnership or a cohabiting couple (same-sex or opposite-sex), and one partner has left and is unlikely to return because of violence or threats of violence by the other towards them or a member of the family living with them. The landlord must satisfy the court that they have served notice of the proceedings for possession on the partner who has left the home, or that they have taken reasonable steps to do this, or if not, that they have taken reasonable steps to do so or can argue it is just and equitable to dispense with the notice requirements (s.150 HA 1996). Ground 14A is the same as Ground 2A in Schedule 2 of the HA 1985 for secure tenants. It is important to note that in order for the domestic violence ground to be satisfied, it must be the real and effective reason the partner left, not just one amongst a number of reasons (*Camden LBC v Mallet [2001]* 33 HLR, CA)

Ground 14Z – Offence during a riot

Following the riots in 2011 across a number of cities in England the Government added the above discretionary ground. This related to a situation where the tenant or an adult residing in the dwelling-house has been convicted of an indictable offence which took place during, and at the scene of a riot in the UK. The offence must have been committed on or after 13 May 2014. A riot is defined as where 12 or more persons, who are present together, use or threaten unlawful violence for a common purpose and the conduct of them (taken together) is such as would cause a person of reasonable firmness present at the scene to fear for their personal safety – S.1 Public Order Act 1986.

Question

What is meant by the structured discretion?

Suggested answer

The courts in England (and Wales) since 2004, have been required by the provisions of s.9A of the HA 1988 (mirrored in s.85A HA 1985 for secure tenants for possession under Ground 2) to consider in particular:

(a) the effect that the nuisance or annoyance has had on persons other than the person against whom the order is sought;

(b) any continuing effect the nuisance or annoyance is likely to have on such persons; and

(c) the effect that the nuisance or annoyance would be likely to have on such persons if the conduct is repeated. [v]

In *Moat Housing Group – South Ltd v Harris and Hartless [2005]* HLR 33, CA, an outright possession order was made against a mother and her four children who were aged between 6-14 because of a nuisance and threats caused by the mother and two of her children, and her partner who was a non-resident. The nuisance had consisted of vandalism, graffiti, littering, bullying, swearing and threats to other residents.

In the case of *London and Quadrant Housing Trust v Root [2005]* HLR 28, CA, a car repair business was being run from the tenant's front garden, causing nuisance due to litter and noise, which was in breach of the terms of the tenancy agreement. Threats and verbal abuse had been aimed at any neighbours who complained about the noise. An outright possession order was upheld by the court, who took into account the conduct and attitude of the tenant in breaching her tenancy agreement.

The court has been shown to take a strong line when a tenant or members of his family have been guilty of racial abuse of their neighbours, and more likely to make an outright possession order rather than a suspended order (*West Kent HA v Davies [1999]* 31 HLR 415).

Question

When is Ground 15 relevant?

Suggested answer

Ground 15 – Recovery because of furniture deterioration

In a situation where the landlord has provided furniture under the tenancy, if he/she can show that the furniture has deteriorated due to ill-treatment by the tenant, or any other person residing in the dwelling-house, this ground can be used. Once again, where the ill-treatment was due to the actions of a lodger or sub-tenant, the landlord must show that the tenant has not taken such steps as he ought reasonably to have taken to remove that person.

Question

When does Ground 16 kick in?

Suggested answer

Ground 16 – Recovery from a former employee

In some situations the landlord may have been the employer of the tenant, with the tenancy granted with the job as a package. Once the employment comes to an end the landlord will have the right to recover the property. It is not necessary for the landlord to show that he/she needs the property for another employee, but this may have some bearing when it comes to influencing the court's decision in exercising its discretion on reasonableness.

Question

When does Ground 17 apply?

Suggested answer

Ground 17 – Recovery for false statements

If a tenant (or a person acting in their name) is shown to have knowingly or recklessly made a false statement which induced the landlord to grant the tenancy, the landlord will be able to recover the property (mirrored in Ground 5, Schedule 2 HA 1985).

Note - Notice periods have been extended due to Covid-19 but likely to revert back as the situation returns back to normal

Chapter 6

Homelessness

Question

What is the current legislation dealing with homelessness?

Suggested answer

The current statute covering homelessness in England and Wales is the Homelessness Reduction Act 2017 (HRA 2017)

Question
Who is considered to be homeless under the HRA 2017?

Suggested answer

A person is legally defined as homeless if:

- They have no accommodation available in the UK or abroad.
- They have no legal right to occupy the accommodation.
- They have a split household and accommodation is not available for the whole household.
- It is unreasonable to continue to occupy their accommodation.
- They are at risk of violence from any person
- They are unable to secure entry to their accommodation.

- They live in a moveable structure but have no place to put it. [vi]

Question

What is the meaning of "threatened with homelessness" under S.1 of the HRM 2017?

Suggested answer

If an applicant makes a homeless application on or after 3 April 2018, this means under the Act that they are threatened with homelessness, if it is likely to be the case that they will become homeless within 56 days.

Also, where a person has been given a valid Section 21 notice relating to their only accommodation, they are also threatened with homelessness if this notice is due to expire within 56 days.

Where a person made a homeless application before 3 April 2018, they would be threatened with homelessness if they were likely to become homeless within 28 days.

Question

What is the duty to provide advisory services under S.2 of the HRM 2017?

Suggested answer

The duty to provide advisory services extended the existing duty of local authorities to provide free advice and information on homelessness, to anyone in their local authority area. This will include advice and information on preventing homelessness, securing accommodation when homeless, the rights of homeless people or those who are threatened with homelessness. This advice is also supposed to be tailored for the needs of vulnerable groups such as care leavers, victims of domestic abuse, people released from prison or youth detention accommodation, former members of the armed services, people leaving hospital and those suffering from a mental illness or impairment. [vii]

Question

What is the duty to assess all eligible applicants' cases and agree a plan under S.3?

Suggested answer

Section 3 lays out the process local authorities must, regardless of priority need, agree a homelessness plan. This will involve carrying out an assessment in all cases where an applicant is homeless, or at the risk of becoming homeless. After this assessment the council must work with the person who has applied for assistance, to agree the actions that both parties need to take to make sure the person has, or is able to, retain suitable accommodation.

Question

What is meant by the duty in cases of threatened homelessness under S.4?

Suggested answer

Section 4 of the HRM 2017 lays out the duty, that councils should take reasonable steps to prevent homelessness for any individual at risk of homelessness, regardless of priority need. This will consist of helping an individual stay in their current accommodation, or help them to find a new place to live in. This links with Section 1, as the duty applies to applicants who are considered as being threatened with homelessness 56 days before they are likely to become homeless. Section 4 outlines the circumstances where the local authority has a duty to prevent homelessness, which may be brought to an end by the service of a written notice. This will include where the local authority is satisfied that suitable accommodation has been secured where there is a reasonable prospect of that accommodation being retained for six months (or for a longer period up to a maximum of 12 months if allowed for in regulations).

The statutory guidance gives a few examples of reasonable steps that could be taken by the authority to save the applicant's home:

- o   attempting mediation/conciliation where an applicant is threatened with parent/family exclusion;
- o   assessing whether applicants with rent arrears might be entitled to discretionary housing payments
- o   assisting people at risk of violence and abuse wishing to stay safely in their home through provision of 'sanctuary' or other measures. [viii]

Question

What is meant by Section 5 - duties owed to those who are homeless?

Suggested answer

Local authorities have a duty under section 5 to relieve homelessness for all eligible households, regardless of priority need. This will consist of a local authority taking reasonable steps to help the applicant secure suitable accommodation for any eligible person who is homeless, this duty lasts for up to 56 days. This may be relevant where help is needed for a rent deposit or debt advice. This is a change from the current interim accommodation duty owed by councils to homeless applicants who are in priority need.

Question

What is duty to secure accommodation under Section 6?

Suggested answer

This duty works alongside the prevention and relief duties set out in sections 4 and 5. Local authorities have the flexibility to assist in trying to resolve housing issues by providing support and advice to households. Those households would then be responsible for securing their own accommodation. Local authorities can still help find accommodation for applicants if this is appropriate, which must be deemed suitable.

Question

What is meant by the deliberate and unreasonable refusal to co-operate: duty upon giving notice under Section 7?

Suggested answer

Section 7 lays out the actions a local authority can take if an applicant who is homeless, or threatened with homelessness, deliberately and unreasonably refuses to take any steps that are laid out in the agreed personalised plan. In addition, it also outlines the procedure and duties that will bind the applicant who is homeless, where he/she refuses at the relief stage, a suitable final offer of accommodation. Priority need applicants who fail to cooperate will however, remain eligible for an offer of settled accommodation.

Question

What is meant by Section 8: Local connection of a care leaver?

Suggested answer

Section 8 deals with the duty to care leavers (young person leaving care) and makes it easier to show they have a local connection with the area. Detailed codes of guidance have been produced by the government for local authorities. [ix]

Question

What is the duty under Section 9 - Reviews?

Suggested answer

Section 9 enables an applicant to request a review of their local authority's decision on homelessness.

Question

What is the duty under Section10: Duty of public authority to refer cases to a local housing authority?

Suggested answer

This section requires public authorities to notify a local authority of service users they think may be homeless or at risk of becoming homeless. This is set out in regulations [x]. For this to happen a public authority must gain the consent of the person before they are able to refer them, and individuals will be allowed to choose which council they are referred to.

Question

What does Section11 deal with?

Suggested answer

Section 11 has enabled mandatory Codes of Practice to be produced by the Secretary of State to deal with local authorities' functions dealing with homelessness or homelessness prevention. Future codes may be added for other specific issues.

Question

What is the duty under Section 12: Suitability of private rented sector accommodation?

Suggested answer

Section 12 requires that local authorities must ensure that certain suitability requirements are satisfied when they secure accommodation for vulnerable households in the private rented sector.

Chapter 7

Procedure to be followed by a landlord or mortgagee when seeking possession of premises

Question

Is there a protocol governing possession claims based on Rent Arrears and how is it applied?

Suggested answer

There is a Pre-action Protocol for Possession Claims based on Rent Arrears. It is aimed at social landlords such as LHAs, RSLs, PRPs and HATs. The Protocol's purpose is to encourage more pre-action contact between landlords and tenants and make more effective use of court time where claims are based on rent arrears. The Protocol does not apply to long leases or claims for possession where there is no security of tenure. Under the Protocol social landlords must take all reasonable steps to avoid litigation.

The landlord must contact the tenant as soon as reasonably possible after he actually goes into arrears with his/her rent. The landlord should discuss what caused the tenant to go into arrears, their financial position and benefit entitlement, and whether he/she is able to repay arrears. The landlord should offer to help the tenant claim housing benefit if eligible. Guidance is produced as part of the Protocol by what is currently the Department for Levelling Up, Housing and Communities, that social landlords need to comply with.

Where a landlord decides to instigate possession proceedings, they should provide the tenant with an up-to-date rent statement no later than 10 days before the hearing. In addition, the landlord should disclose their knowledge of the tenant's situation regarding housing benefit. Also, the landlord is required to let the tenant know of the hearing and advise them to attend the hearing and keep a record of this advice.

It is important to note that the Protocol states that possession proceedings should not be started in a situation where rent arrears are increasing due to a delay in housing benefit. Instead, it should apply where rent arrears are due to the fault of the tenant, in not making payment for sums not actually covered by housing benefit.

After possession proceedings have begun, the court may need proof from the parties that they have made some effort to try to resolve the dispute through discussion and negotiation before proceedings have started. A claim may be adjourned, struck out or dismissed (except where a claim is brought only on mandatory grounds). In the alternative, if the landlord unreasonably fails to stick to the terms of the Protocol, there may be costs penalties. For tenants, if they do nor comply with the Protocol this may also be taken into consideration by the court as a factor in deciding on whether an order should be made.

Question

What is the pre-action Protocol covering Possession Claims based on Mortgage or Home Purchase Plan Arrears in Respect of Residential Property?

Suggested answer

This Protocol is aimed at making sure mortgagees ("lenders") an mortgagors ("borrowers") act fairly and reasonably with each other when dealing with arrears. The aim or purpose of the Protocol is to encourage more pre-action contact between the parties so that they can try and reach agreement, and avoid unnecessary court action.
The Protocol applies to arrears on:
(a) first charge residential mortgages and home purchase plans regulated by the Financial Standards Authority (FSA) under the Financial Services and Markets Act 2000;
(b) second charge mortgages over residential property and other secured loans regulated under the Consumer Credit Act 1974 on residential property; and
(c) unregulated residential mortgages.
The Protocol applies to possession claims which include a money claim as well.

There is detailed guidance in the Protocol for the lender on what information he/she should provide and steps they should take to try to avoid a possession claim. In addition, there are obligations placed on the borrower to act reasonably in facilitating an agreement. In a situation where the lender reaches the decision that a possession claim is unavoidable, he/she must give the borrower notice of the reasons why they have come to this decision, 5 days before they start proceedings.

Question

How does a claimant bring a possession claim?

Suggested answer

A claimant can bring a possession claim at any County Court hearing centre. It is advisable though, to bring a claim at the County Court hearing centre which covers the address where the land is based (PD 55A, para 5.3). A possession claim will only usually be brought in the High Court where there are complicated disputes of fact, points of law of general importance. Other situations would be where there are claims against trespassers where there is a substantial risk of public disturbance or serious harm to persons or property which, call for immediate determination (PD 55A, para 1.3). Where a claim is started in the High Court, then, under CPR, r55.3(2) a claimant is required to file a certificate stating the reasons for bringing his/her claim in the High Court (verified by a Statement of Truth). If the claim is brought in inappropriately in the High Court there will be cost penalties.

Question

What is the appropriate claim form?

Suggested answer

The claimant needs to use the appropriate claim form and particulars of claim form (PD 55A, para 1.5). This will be one of the following:-

N5 – claim form for possession of property;
N5A – claim form for relief against forfeiture; and
N5B – claim form for possession of property (accelerated procedure) (assured shorthold
tenancy).

A claimant can use a single claim form to start all claims which can be disposed of in the same proceedings. Thus, possession claims can include other issues such as rent arrears.

Question

What is required along with the claim form?

Suggested answer

The claimant needs to use the correct particulars of claim form which must be filed and served with the claim form. The relevant forms are set out in PD4, para 3.1 and are:-

N119 – particulars of claim for possession (rented residential premises);
N120 – particulars of claim for possession (mortgaged residential premises); and
N121 – particulars of claim for possession (trespassers).

CPR r16.4 lays out the general contents of the particulars of claim. There is further guidance on the contents of different types of possession claims. Generally the particulars of claim in any possession proceedings must:-

(a) identify the land to which the claim relates;
(b) state whether the claim relates to residential property;
(c) state the grounds on which possession is claimed;
(d) give full details of any mortgage or tenancy agreement; and
(e) give details of every person who, to the best of the claimant's knowledge, is in possession of the property.

Question

Are there additional requirements for residential property?

Suggested answer

PD 55, para 2.3 sets out what must be in the particulars of claim in the case of tenancies of residential property, where the claim includes a claim for non-payment of rent. This will consist of:-

(a) the amount due at the start of the proceedings;
(b) a schedule of the dates when the arrears of rent arose, all amounts of rent due, the dates and amounts of all payments made, and a running total of the arrears;
(c) the daily rate of any rent and interest;
(d) any previous steps taken to recover the arrears of rent with full details of any court proceedings; and
(e) any relevant information about the defendant's circumstances, in particular details of whether he is on social security benefits and whether any benefit payments are made direct to the claimant.
In addition, if the claimant wishes to rely on a history of arrears which is longer than two years, he should state this in his particulars and exhibit a full (or longer) schedule to a witness statement (PD 55A, para 2.3A).
If the claimant knows of any person (including a mortgagee) entitled to claim relief against
forfeiture as underlessee, the particulars of claim must state the name and address of that person; and the claimant must file a copy of the particulars of claim for service on him (PD 55A, para 2.4). If the claim for possession relates to the conduct of the tenant or relies on a statutory ground or grounds for possession, the particulars of claim must state details of the conduct alleged and specify the ground or grounds relied on (PD 55A, para 2.4A and 2.4B).[xi]

A claimant who is seeking possession based solely on rent arrears grounds or mortgage arrears can issue the claim on line (CPR, r55.10A and PD 55B).

Question

What happens in possession claims brought by mortgagees?

Suggested answer

Where a mortgagee brings a possession claim in relation to residential property PD 55A, para 2.5 states that the particulars of claim must also set out the following:-

(a) whether a Class F land charge applies, or a notice under the Matrimonial Homes Act 1967 or 1983 respectively has been registered, or a notice under the Family Law Act 1996 (if any of the provisions apply, the claimant will have to serve notice of the claim on the persons on whose behalf the registration or notice was entered);
(b) the mortgage account, including the amount of the advance, any periodic repayments and interest, and the amount needed to redeem the mortgage, including the costs of redeeming;
(c) if the mortgage is a regulated consumer credit agreement, the total amount outstanding; and
(d) the rate of interest payable and any changes since commencement of the mortgage,

immediately before any arrears accrued and at the commencement of proceedings.

In a similar situation as with rent arrears, if the claim is brought for mortgage arrears, PD 55A, para 2.5 requires the particulars of claim to set out in a schedule the dates when the arrears arose, all amounts due, the dates and amounts of all payments made, and a running total of the arrears.

There are similar requirements as with rent arrears to detail benefits provisions and previous steps taken by the claimant to recover the arrears (PD 55A, para 2.5(6) and (8)). Additionally, further details relating to regulated consumer credit loans will be required (PD 55, para 2.5(4), (5)).

Where a mortgagee is seeking possession of residential property he/she must send a notice to the LHA, to any registered proprietor (other than the claimant) of a registered charge over the property, and to the property addressed to 'the tenant or the occupier' within five days of receiving notification of the hearing by the court, giving details of the claim and the hearing (CPR, r55.10). The claimant will need to produce a copy of the notice and evidence of service at the hearing.

Question

How are possession claims against trespassers brought?

Suggested answer

A trespasser in these situations can be described as someone who entered or remained on the land without consent of a person who was entitled to possession of that land. This does not include a tenant or sub-tenant whose tenancy is terminated. Where a claim is against a trespasser and the claimant does not know his or her name, then under CPR, r55.3 (4) the claim must be brought against 'persons unknown' (on top of any other named defendants). Within the particulars of claim against trespassers, the claimant must state their interest in the land, or the nature of his/her right to claim possession, and under PD 55A, para 2.6, the circumstances in which it has been occupied without licence or consent.

A claimant may, in certain circumstances, who has an immediate right to possession of the property, and who acted quickly (within 28 days), when finding out about trespassers on the land, can use the provisions set out in in Section III to obtain an IPO (Interim Possession Order) against the trespasser under CPR, rr 55.20–55.28. The defendant is required under the IPO to vacate the property within 24 hours of the service of the order. If the defendant will not leave the property as required by the order this will constitute and offence. A full hearing of the claim will take place not less than 7 days after and if the claimant is found not to be justified in bringing a claim, then the defendant will be entitled to reinstatement and damages.

Question

How are possession claims brought in cases involving demoted tenancies by a HAT or LHA?

Suggested answer

Where a possession claim is brought against demoted tenants by a HAT or LHA, the particulars of claim must also include a copy of the notice to the tenant served under s.143E of the 1996 Act (PD 55A, para 2.7). CPR Part 55 sets out amended procedures where the landlord is seeking a demotion order in the course of possession proceedings.

In situations where the landlord is only seeking a demotion order, the correct procedure is set out in CPR, rr 65.14–65.19 (Proceedings relating to anti-social behaviour and harassment) and claim form N6 (similar to procedure for CPR Part 55).

Question

How does the court arrange the hearing date?

Suggested answer

The county court will fix a date for the hearing when it issues the claim form. Normally this will be not less than 28 days, with a hearing set for not more than 8 weeks from the date of issue of the claim form. The claim is normally made at the county court hearing centre which serves the address where the land is situated. Where claims are against trespassers, then a shorter period is set.

Question

How is the defendant served with a claim?

Suggested answer

The landlord (claimant) must serve the defendant (tenant) with the claim form and particulars of claim not less than 21 days before the hearing date. Witness statements must be verified by a statement of truth, which must be filed with the court and served at least 2 days before the hearing (CPR, r55.8(4)). The time limits differ in the case of claims brought against trespassers who are occupying residential property. In these cases the trespasser must be served with the claim form, particulars of claim and witness statements if there are any, not less than 5 days before the hearing (CPR, r 55.5(2), (3). There are options for service. The court can arrange for service themselves, or the claimant can arrange service of the documents. Where the claimant serves the claim form and particulars of claim, he/she must provide a certificate of service at the hearing (CPR, r 55.8(6)). Where claims are brought against trespassers where there are 'persons unknown', CPR, r 55.6 sets out procedures for service.[xii] This includes pinning copies of the documents to the main door of the property, putting copies in transparent envelopes pushed through the letter box and attach copies to stakes placed on the land where they are visible.

Question

What is the procedure for the defendant's response?

Suggested answer

The defendant should received the claim form along with the defence form which will contain notes explaining the procedure in submitting a defence. The defence form will differ depending on the status of the defendant. The details of the forms are contained in PD 55A, para 1.5). These are:-

- N11 defence form;
- N11B defence form (accelerated possession procedure) (assured shorthold tenancy);
- N11M defence form (mortgaged residential premises); and
- N11R defence form (rented residential premises).

The defendant is not required to send an acknowledgement of receipt of service of the claim. He/she does need to file their defence within 14 days of service of the claim if they wish to issue a defence.

They may still attend the hearing even where they have failed to file a defence but could suffer cost penalties (CPR r 55.7). A trespasser who is the defendant, does not need to file a defence.

In a possession claim, there is no possibility of obtaining a default judgment because the court must be satisfied that the landlord has made out his claim fully before an order can be made. Defences against the claim could include arguments such as:-

- ✓ The claimant landlord has not served the correct notice;
- ✓ There are no arrears outstanding.

It is common for the defendant tenant to pursue a counter-claim for damages for disrepair of the premises (s.11 LTA 1985). Another defence could be for breach of the covenant of quiet enjoyment (CPR, Part 20). Tactically, the defendant should include such counter-claims as part of his/her defence rather than needing to seek the permission of the court to bring a separate counter-claim.

Question

What happens at the hearing?

Suggested answer

There are miscellaneous provisions in Part 39 of the CPR which deal with hearings. These provisions take account of Article 6 (right to a public hearing), Article 8 (right to private life and correspondence) and Article 14 (prohibiting discrimination) of the European Convention on Human Rights and the Human Rights Act. Under rule 39.2(3) a judge has the discretion to hold a hearing in private if a case concerns confidential information (including any personal financial matters (r 39(2) 3 (c)). This could include claims involving rent or mortgage arrears repossession claims (PD 39). This means most possession claims would be held in private.

At the hearing itself (or an adjourned hearing) the court may do one of two things usually, either decide the claim or give case management directions for the case. If the parties are in disagreement over the substantial grounds of challenge then the directions given will also include which track the claim is to be allocated.

Allocation of claims –

- Possession claims will be allocated to the small claims track if all parties agree and treated as a fast track claim, but will have discretion over trial costs, which must not go above the value of the claim that is recoverable if the value of the claim was up to £30,000 (CPR r.55.9).
- More help and guidance on deciding which track a claim should be allocated to are given in CPR r. 28.8 with more factors to take into account for a possession claim found in

r.55.9(1). This other factors could include the amount in arrears, the importance of the defendant keeping possession and the claimant obtaining it and the conduct of the defendant.
- The county courts will usually use a system listing possession claims brought by social landlords together, but list separately possession claims from private sector landlords and mortgage repossession claims.
- Many defendants do not attend the hearing of the claim and the lists are dealt with in private but the court must be satisfied that the grounds for possession were established, and the correct notice given (i.e. notice to quit or notice seeking possession) was served. In claims where the court has discretion, it should have been reasonable to have made the possession order.
- In cases where the court actually hears a claim, the evidence must be up to date on matters such as benefits, arrears and other factors.

Question

What is Section II of CPR Part 55?

Suggested answer

Section II of the CPR 55 deals with accelerated possession claims against Assured Shorthold Tenants. This allows landlords to use a fast process for dealing with possession claims usually through any County Court hearing centre using Section 21 of the HA 1988. This is dependent on meeting certain conditions found in CPR r 55.12 which are:

(a) the tenancy was entered into on or after 15 January 1989;

(b) the only purpose of the claim is to recover possession, not any other claim such as rent arrears is being made;

(c) the tenancy did not immediately continue straight after an Assured Tenancy which was not an Assured Shorthold tenancy;

(d) the tenancy should meet the conditions set out in s.19 or s.20(1)(a) to (c) of the HA 1988 (Assured Shorthold tenancies pre and post HA 1996);

(e) that there is a written agreement in relation to this or a previous tenancy of the property; and

(f) a notice under S.21(1) or S.21(4) of the HA 1988 was given to the tenant (landlord can obtain a possession order without any fault of the tenant once the proper notice has been served). This has been the subject of recent debate.

Question

Can the accelerated possession procedure be used against demoted Assured Shorthold Tenants?

Suggested answer

Yes, this procedure can be used against a demoted assured shorthold tenant. In these cases the only conditions that will apply are (b) and (f).

Question

Does the government have any proposals to change 'no fault' section 21 evictions?

Suggested answer

Yes, the government has introduced a White Paper, A Fairer Private Rented Sector on 16 June 2022. This set out proposals to abolish section 21 evictions in the private sector and in the background briefing, "introduce a simpler, more secure tenancy structure". In the Queens Speech 2022 the government promised to introduce a Renters Reform Bill in the 2022-23 parliamentary session.

A tenancy will only end if the tenant him/herself brings it to an end or if the landlord has a valid ground for possession. There is apparently an intention by government to reform the grounds for possession to make sure landlords have an effective means to gain possession or their properties when they need to. The preamble discusses the intention to create new grounds to allow landlords to sell or move close family members into the property. Reference is made to strengthen grounds concerning persistent rent arrears and anti-social behaviour.[xiii]

Question

Has the Tenant a defence against an accelerated possession claim?

Suggested answer

A tenant who wants to oppose such a claim or seek a postponement of possession must file a defence using Form N11B. He/she must file a defence with 14 days after service of the claim (CPR, r.55.14). The tenant, if they do not file a defence within 14 days, this could result in the claimant filing a written request for a possession order. If the claimant files a defence, the court will send a copy to the claimant and the case is sent to a judge. The judge can then make an order for possession and there will not be a requirement for the parties to attend court if the claim is clearly made out. Conversely, if the judge is not satisfied that the claim is made out, he can arrange a date for the hearing and case management directions made, or he/she can strike out the claim if s/he believes the claim fails to disclose any reasonable grounds for bringing the claim (CPR rr 55.16 and 55.17). It is open to the claimant to apply to have the claim restored within 28 days after s/he has been served with the order and reasons for the claim being struck out.

It is important to note that if the correct notice has not been served or the notice is defective, the claim will fail as set out currently under s.21 HA 1988. In *Manel v Memon (2001) 33 HLR 235, CA,* failure to include notes advising on the need to take legal advice, meant the notice was invalid.

Question

Can the Tenant seek a postponement of possession?

Suggested answer

The tenant/defendant can seek a postponement of the possession order on the ground of exceptional hardship. A hearing will then be held unless the landlord/claimant has made clear he/she would not object to postponement of possession. If the judge is satisfied that exceptional hardship would result by requiring possession of the property on the date set out in the order (14 days normally), s/he can give a date 6 weeks after the order was made (CPR, r55.18). This discretion is found under S.89 HA 1980.

Question

What are the deciding factors for the judge when considering different types of possessions orders?

Suggested answer

Once a claimant has made his/her case for possession, the type of order a judge can make will depend on a number of factors which would include:-

- The type of occupancy the tenant has; and
- which statutory scheme.

The court may decide not to make any order in certain cases where it has the discretion. In such situations the judge may decide to adjourn any proceedings, with or without terms.

Examples

Possession orders may be:-

- Immediate (take effect straightaway) – usually made against a trespasser;
- Outright or absolute - (take effect within 14 days unless a tenant claims exceptional hardship in which case an order may be postponed). This order can be used against a tenant/occupier who has no security of tenure such as an assured shorthold tenant or where the claimant has a mandatory right of possession;

- Suspended – These are generally used where the court has discretion. Possession may be ordered within 28 days suspended on terms that the defendant complies with conditions set (if conditions are not met the claimant can apply for a warrant of execution).
- Postponed on terms – Under form N28A grants possession postponed on terms. In these situations no date for possession is set out in the order and a date will be fixed by the court after the application is made by the claimant. In these cases the claimant will only be entitled to the court for a possession if the claimant has breached the payment terms, and they have followed the procedure correctly (Para 10.3 PD 55A). This requires the claimant to give written notice in advance of between 14 days and 3 months before the application, that needs to be given to the tenant of his/her intention to apply for an order that gives a fixed date for possession. This written notice must -
    - Set out the claimant's intention to apply for an order;
    - Set out the amount of current arrears;
    - Set out how the defendant has failed to comply with the order;
    - Request a reply from the defendant within 7 days with reasons why he/she disagrees with the amount of arrears; and;

> ➤ Inform the defendant of his/her right to apply to the court for a further postponement of the date for possession or to stay or suspend enforcement.

Where a defendant agrees with the arrears set out in the order, he/she must give reasons why payments have not been made when replying. Evidence of payments or credits made should be provided if he/she disagrees with the amount quoted. Judges in the county courts generally use form N28A when they grant possession orders regarding assured and secure tenants, now extended where landlords seek to bring to an end secure, assured, introductory and demoted tenancies. The latter changes were due to amendments in legislation (s.299 and Schedule 11 to the Housing and Regeneration Act 2008, which amended s.82 of the Housing Act 1985, ss 5 and 21 of the Housing Act 1988 and ss.127 and 143 of the Housing Act 1996). This made it the case that a landlord wanting to terminate one of the tenancies mentioned, must get a court order for possession and ensure it is executed by obtaining a warrant for possession and have the tenant evicted by court bailiffs.

Question

How will the courts use their discretionary powers in possessions orders?

Suggested answer

The court has a wide discretion when it comes to possession proceedings. This includes the discretion to:-

- Adjourn the possession proceedings;
- If the possession order is made, to stay or suspend execution of the order; or
- Postpone the date of possession to a date agreed by the court.

When considering whether it is reasonable or not to make an order for possession, a court will consider a number of factors, such as the tenant's record of paying their rent, his/her behaviour and past arrears and reasons (apart for mandatory Ground 8 for Assured Tenants where there is no discretion). Several tenants may be experiencing delays in receiving their housing benefit to pay rent

Question

How do the courts use their discretion in anti-social behaviour possession claims?

Suggested answer

The relevant statutory provisions governing this area are:-

Section 85A of the Housing Act:-

Proceedings for possession [on non-absolute grounds]: anti-social behaviour

(1) This section applies if the court is considering under section 84(2)(a) whether it is reasonable to make an order for possession on ground 2 set out in Part 1 of Schedule 2 (conduct of tenant or other person).

(2) The court must consider, in particular—

(a) the effect that the nuisance or annoyance has had on persons other than the person against whom the order is sought;

(b any continuing effect the nuisance or annoyance is likely to have on such persons;

(c) the effect that the nuisance or annoyance would be likely to have on such persons if the conduct is repeated.

Section 9A of the Housing Act 1988:-

Proceedings for possession [on non-absolute grounds]: anti-social behaviour

(1) This section applies if the court is considering under section 7(4) whether it is reasonable to make an order for possession on ground 14 set out in Part 2 of Schedule 2 (conduct of tenant or other person).

(2) The court must consider, in particular—

(a)the effect that the nuisance or annoyance has had on persons other than the person against whom the order is sought;

(b) any continuing effect the nuisance or annoyance is likely to have on such persons;

(c) the effect that the nuisance or annoyance would be likely to have on such persons if the conduct is repeated.

An example of how the courts apply this discretion is best explained through relevant caselaw -

Solon South West Housing Association Ltd v James
[2004] All ER (D) 328, CA. In this case the court
upheld an order for immediate possession as the
defendant had a 2-year history of terrorising their
neighbours. The factors that influenced the judge
included the unrepentant nature of the defendant for
his actions, and fear of witnesses to come forward for
fear of reprisals against them.

Sheffield City Council v Shaw [2007] HLR 25, CA. In
this case the defendant had become obsessed with
his neighbour's 12-year old daughter, and had
continued to stalk and harass her over a number of
years, including a threat to kill her. He was convicted
for harassment, which resulted in a restraining order
and an ASBO against him (both of these he
breached). The defendant apologised for his
behaviour at the subsequent trial and psychiatric
evidence indicated with help he could change his
behaviour. Based on this evidence, the judge made a
suspended possession order. The landlord appealed
against this decision, one of the grounds being that
insufficient weight had been given to the fear and
apprehension of the victim in this case, and the
defendant's behaviour could reoccur in the future.
The Court dismissed their appeal and held that past
conduct should not outweigh future optimism. It is
interesting to note that the case the landlord relied
upon for his argument, *Lambeth LBC v Howard*
(2001) 33 HLR 58, CA, had reached a different
decision based on the facts. In this latter case, the
defendant had improved his behaviour, but had

refused to acknowledge the harm he had caused by his conduct. In *Lambeth LBC v Howard* however, he had, after many years, realised his behaviour was wrong and had apologised and sought psychiatric help.

British Anzani (Felixstowe) Ltd v International Marine Management (UK) Ltd [1980] QB 137. Where the tenant has a valid counter-claim to the arrears, this may be used to cancel the arrears.

Question

How do the courts approach applying the mandatory grounds of possession claims?

Suggested answer

When it comes to the mandatory grounds for possession, the courts have more restricted powers and must follow the relevant mandatory ground where the claimant makes a strong case. These are governed by the RA 1977 in the case of regulated tenants, and Part 1 of Schedule 2 to the HA 1988 or Section 21 (subject to recent changes to Section 21) of the HA 1988, in the case of assured or assured shorthold tenants. It is important to state that the claimant will not get an order for possession under the relevant ground, if they have not properly established a case, or the procedure has not been correctly followed (*Mountain v Hastings [1995]* 25 HLR 427, CA).

Question

What happens where a mortgagee (Lender) wishes to seek possession of a property from a mortgagor (Borrower)?

Suggested answer

A mortgagee will usually have a common law right to possession of a mortgaged property covered by a term in the mortgage agreement that will entitle them to exercise his/her right of possession if the mortgagor breaches a fundamental term of the agreement. It is however important to point out that this power, is subject to statutory protection under the Administration of Justice Act 1970 and 1973 (AJA) in the case of residential mortgages, and where it is a regulated agreement, the Consumer Credit Act 1974 (CCA). Section 36 of the AJA (as amended by S.8 of the AJA 1973) gives the power to the court to adjourn the possession proceedings, or stay or suspend the application of the order, or postpone the possession date if the courts believes the mortgagor is able to pay off the arrears and sums overdue on the mortgage, within a reasonable period of time. It is important to note that a court cannot suspend an order under S.36 if there is no real prospect that the mortgagor will be able to reduce the arrears (*Abbey National Mortgages v Barnard [1996]* 71 P & CR 257 CA). The Mortgages Pre-action Protocol [xiv] aims to help reduce claims and reach an equitable resolution. Some loans may still be covered by the CCA[xv] which give the courts wider powers on rescheduling of repayments etc.

Question

What is the Mortgage Repossessions (Protection of Tenants etc) Act 2010?

Suggested answer

The Mortgage Repossessions (Protection of Tenants etc) Act 2010, offers protection to tenants by giving them the right to be heard at possession hearings, gives courts and judges authority to take tenants' needs into account, and allows possession to be postponed by up to two months so that the tenant can find an alternative home. This Act enables unauthorised tenants to apply to the courts in order to delay repossession for up to 2 months provided:-

- The court has not already allowed an extension of time when the possession order was made.
- The tenant has asked the mortgage lender to agree to delay the execution of the warrant for possession and it has been refused.

In such cases the court can take into account whether the tenant has breached the terms of the unauthorised tenancy (i.e. rent arrears or anti-social behaviour), and also has the power to order a tenant to pay rent outstanding, to the lender *without creating a tenancy between the lender and tenant.*

Question

How do possessions operate in the case of forfeiture of a long lease?

Suggested answer

A long leaseholder who defaults on certain terms of his/her lease, may face possession proceedings. This could come about through non-payment of ground rent or service charges, or breach of another fundamental term/s of their lease. Section 2 of the Protection from Eviction Act 1977(PEA 1977) requires that forfeiture proceedings against a person who occupies a residential premises should be instigated through court proceedings. The County Court has powers granted through S.138 of the County Courts Act 1984 (CCA 1984) as amended, when it comes to forfeiture for rent arrears, or under S.146(2) of the Law of Property Act (LPA)1925, when it comes to other breaches, to grant relief against forfeiture. When it comes to rent arrears claims, the court has powers under s.138 CCA 1984, to suspend a possession order for a minimum of 4 weeks to allow the lessee the opportunity to pay off any arrears. There is still the possibility for the lessee to apply for relief up to 6 months after possession has been granted, even where he/she defaults on payment of arrears. In cases where a there are breaches other than arrears of rent., S.146(2) of the LPA 1925 give the court power to grant relief on conditions it deems appropriate. The court will take into account various factors in deciding to grant relief which will likely be:-

- Nature and seriousness of the breach;
- Conduct of parties;
- Value of the property; and
- Extent of any damage caused by the breach and any losses suffered by the tenant in failing to grant relief.

The court is at liberty to impose terms in relation to costs, expenses, damages or compensation or penalties, which can include the granting of an injunction to restrain any future breaches (LPA 1925 S. 146(2)).

Question

What happens in cases of possession orders against trespassers?

Suggested answer

Where a possession order is made against a trespasser, this will normally take immediate effect. The court has to make an immediate order (unless the claimant suggests other action) and has no discretion to suspend an order, or give time for the trespasser to vacate a property for reason of exceptional hardship.

Question

How does a suspended order operate?

Suggested answer

A suspended order may be used by the court where there has been an eviction hearing and the court has decided to apply a suspended order against a tenant who is in rent arrears. The court will impose certain conditions on the tenant to pay arrears of rent (form N28 is used). In these cases the tenancy will continue to exist provided the tenant met the conditions set. Examples of possible conditions are given on the Shelter website namely:-

- ✓ paying your normal rent plus a set amount towards rent arrears

- ✓ stopping any antisocial behaviour

If the tenant breaks the terms, a landlord can apply for a bailiff's warrant and the bailiff will send a notice with a date for the eviction to occur. A tenant could ask the court to suspend the warrant if they are able to afford to pay the rent plus an amount towards rent arrears. A tenant can use Form N244 to make a request to vary terms of the order, and also use this from to discharge the order if it can be shown arrears have been paid off.

Question

When are postponed orders applied?

Suggested answer

This type of possession order is made by the courts where a tenant is able to pay the current rent as well as an amount towards arrears of rent, within a reasonable time. The courts may base this on the type of landlord, i.e. whether a social landlord or a private sector landlord. This is discussed in Housing

Law and Practice based on analysis of two case decisions[xvi]. In the case of *Lambeth LBC v Henry [2000]* 32 HLR 874 CA, the Court held that paying £1.85 per week off arrears amounting to £2,375 although likely to take 23 years to take off, was not an unreasonable period of time in the case of social landlord tenants. In contrast, in *Taj v Ali [2001]* 33 HLR 27 CA, a Rent Act 1977 (RA 1977) case, the trial judge made a suspended order in connection with arrears owed of £14,500, based on current rent of £49 plus £5 a week off arrears. This would have taken over 55 years to pay off the total rent. The Court of Appeal overturned this decision and held that suspending possession for an indefinite period that 'stretched into the mists of time' was not reasonable and imposed an outright order for possession instead of the suspended order.

Question

What is a tolerated trespasser and how are possession orders applied in these situations?

Suggested answer

A tolerated trespasser is a tenant under a secure or assured periodic tenancy, who does not relinquish his/her possession of the property when the tenancy comes to an end. In *Jones v London Borough of*

Merton [2008] EWCA Civ 660 the court outlines three situations where a tolerated trespasser may exist:-

- They are actively tolerated by the former landlord – when the parties enter into an express agreement that the former landlord will not take action to enforce a possession order if the former tenant meets certain requirements, such as, payment of rent.
- They are passively tolerated by the former landlord – when the former landlord fails to take any action to enforce a possession order and the former tenant remains in possession of the property.
- They are tolerated by the court – when a possession order requested from the court by a former landlord is stayed or suspended by powers of the court.

The current case on this area is *Knowsley Housing Trust v White [2008]* UKHL,70 [2009], where the House of Lords held that assured tenancies did not terminate until the date of the execution of the possession order. This placed some doubt on the concept of the tolerated trespasser. The Housing and Regeneration Act [2008] Sched. 11 which came into force on 20 May 2009, provided that tenancies falling within these Acts (Housing Acts 1985, 1988 and 1996) do not end until the possession order is executed (i.e. actual eviction)[xvii].

As a tolerated trespasser, the ex-tenant no longer had any contractual rights to rely on in bringing a claim against the landlord. A tenant could not rely upon a breach of covenant to repair, or in some tenancies the right to buy, assign or succession, once they became a tolerated trespasser.

CHAPTER 8

How can tenants challenge possession orders

Question

How can a tenant challenge a possession order?

Suggested answer

There are a number of ways a tenant can challenge a possession order. The options available are:-

- apply to have the order set aside as long certain conditions are met;
- lodge an appeal against the order;
- or make an application to stay or suspend an order.

Question

How does a tenant make an application to set aside a possession order?

Suggested answer

The tenant (defendant) who does not attend a hearing can make an application to set aside a possession order. An application can be made under CPR r 3.1 –

case management. The requirements under CPR r 39.3 (Failure to attend the trial) must be adhered to, namely –

(2) Where the court strikes out proceedings, or any part of them, under this rule, it may subsequently restore the proceedings, or that part.

(3) Where a party does not attend and the court gives judgment or makes an order against him, the party who failed to attend may apply for the judgment or order to be set aside

(4) An application under paragraph (2) or paragraph (3) must be supported by evidence.

(5) Where an application is made under paragraph (2) or (3) by a party who failed to attend the trial, the court may grant the application only if the applicant –

(a) acted promptly when he found out that the court had exercised its power to strike out or to enter judgment or make an order against him;
(b) had a good reason for not attending the trial; and
(c) has a reasonable prospect of success at the trial.

In the context of housing possession cases these this would likely apply where a tenant:-

(a) acted promptly on becoming aware of the order;
(b) had a good excuse for not attending the hearing; and
(c) has a reasonable prospect of success at a reconvened trial.

The effect of a possession order being set aside is that the tenancy is restored as if an order had never been made. It is necessary that all three requirements must be met before the courts will set a possession order aside. In some cases a tenant will not attend after being told by a landlord he/she need not attend the hearing, which may be accepted by the court for not attending.

the case of *Akram v Adam* [2005] 1 All ER 741, CA, the defendant/tenant applied to have a possession order set aside that had been made against him in his absence. This was a case under Article 6 ECHR (Right to a fair trial). He claimed that he had not received the claim from, particulars of claim and the notification of the hearing date (sent to him by first-class post as per CPR r 6.2(1)(b)). The defendant argued that the right to notification of the date for the hearing was a fundamental principle of law, and even if service has been effected corrected in line with the rules, the judgement should be set aside as it would otherwise not be compatible with the right to a fair trial under Article 6 ECHR. This argument was rejected by the Court of Appeal who held that in this case service had been correctly effected, judgment could only be set aside based on discretion under CPR r 13.3, and on the facts of the case, as the defence had no merit, there would have been no point in setting aside the judgment. The Court found that Article 6 had not been breached based on the fact that where there was no defence with a real prospect of success or some other compelling reason for a trial. The parties, nor the court, were required to become involved in an expensive and time-consuming charade.

An accelerated possession order (made under CPR r 55.17) can also be set aside of varied under CPR r 55.19. This can either be via an application by a party within 14 days of service of the order, or on the initiative of the court.

Question

How can the tenant appeal against a possession order?

Suggested answer

Where a tenant is not able to apply to set aside a possession order because they are unable to meet the required conditions, he/she may be able to appeal the order. Applying CPR, Part 52, a party to proceedings can appeal to a circuit judge (once permission is agreed by the district judge who heard the case, or if not, just appealing to a district judge). The party (tenant in these circumstances) makes an application using Form N161, and the tenant must show that there is a real prospect of the appeal being successful, or there is some other compelling reason why the appeal should be heard (i.e. judge has made an error in law or incorrectly applied the law in making the order). The tenant needs to file notice within 21 days of the date of the order. In order to prevent the landlord from executing the possession order, the tenant may be advised to make an application, pending any appeal to stay the order.

Question

How can the tenant stay, suspend or discharge a possession order?

Suggested answer

If a tenant wishes to stay or suspend execution of the order, or to postpone the date of possession, they will need to apply to the court. An application can be made using Form N244, at any time before execution of the possession order, to stay or suspend execution of the order, or to postpone the date of possession. Such an application may be made by the former tenant, or by a non-tenant spouse or civil partner who has home rights under the Family Law Act 1996 and remains in occupation of the premises. In addition to the above, personal representatives of a deceased tenant may also make an application (*Austin v Southwark* [2010] 3 WLR 144 UKSC). The landlord/claimant in some cases may apply to vary the terms of a suspended order, where, for instance, new facts were to come to light that indicate that a suspended order should be replaced by an outright order (*Manchester City Council v Finn* [2002] EWCA Civ 1998).

If the tenant is successful in meeting the conditions in a postponed or suspended possession order, the tenant may then apply for the order to be discharged or rescinded under the HA 1985, S.85(4) – HA 1988, S.9(4) – RA 1977, S.100(4).

Question

How does a Landlord/Claimant apply for a warrant for possession?

Suggested answer

The landlord may apply for a warrant for possession where he/she has obtained a possession order, but the tenant remains in the property. He/she will need to make an application using Form N325. The landlord can do this without needing to have leave of the court, at any time up to six years after the date of the possession order. The landlord is not required to give notice to the tenant in the County Court, unless it is specified in the original possession order that no warrant should be issued without the leave of the court. Once the warrant is granted it will be valid for 12 months, to be renewed by the court as necessary. It will be the job of the court bailiffs to enforce the warrant, who will have the power to evict all those in the property. It is usual for the bailiffs to give advance notice to the tenant/defendant and any other occupants of the property, warning them when execution of the warrant will happen using Form N54. It is usual for them to notify the defendant that they can make an application to the court to suspend the warrant. The court has the discretion to stay or suspend the warrant before execution under S.85(2) of the HA 1985 – S.9(2) HA 1988 or S.100(2) RA 1977.

Following any application by the tenant for a stay or suspension of the warrant of execution, the landlord can object to this application by producing new evidence to court (even evidence not produced in the original hearing – *Sheffield City Council v Hopkins [2001]* All ER (D) 196, CA).

Question

What is meant by oppression after a warrant has been issued?

Suggested answer

Once a warrant has been executed it cannot be undone usually. If a late application to set aside the possession order is allowed by the court, however, any warrant would become void. Other possible scenarios for set aside, could be where a tenant can show an executed warrant for possession was obtained by fraud, or where there has been an abuse of process or oppression in its execution. Possible examples of oppression could be maladministration a landlord of a local housing authority.

Question

Is there public funding to defend possession claims?

Suggested answer

There are Housing Possession Court Duty Schemes that provide advice and representation in possession cases. This current scheme is being reviewed and subject to changes in 2023. Shelter provide useful advice and guidance on how these operate (link below) and the Legal Action Group (LAG) produce detailed guidance in this area.

Shelter Legal England – Legal aid for housing and debt problems - Shelter England

INDEX

[i] Housing Law and Practice / College of Law Publishing - © The University of Law 2015 - Gail Price LLB (Hons), LLM, Barrister
[ii] Ibid P.15 (2015)
[iii] HOUSE OF COMMONS BRIEFING PAPER Number 7173 2 September 2018 - Social housing: flexible and fixed-term tenancies (England)
[iv] https://england.shelter.org.uk/professional_resources/legal/renting/other_public_sector_tenancies/introductory_tenancies
[v] Ibid P.24 (2015)
[vi] ss.175-177 Housing Act 1996 as amended by the Homelessness Reduction Act 2018; chapter 6 Homelessness Code of Guidance, MHCLG, Feb 2018 - https://www.shelter.org.uk
[vii] Get in on the Act - Homelessness Reduction Act 2017 / LGA briefing - April 2017
[viii] Homelessness Reduction Act 2017 - Policy and Practice Briefing - Shelter

[ix] Chapter 22: Care leavers - Homelessness code of guidance for local authorities - Guidance - GOV.UK (www.gov.uk)

[x] Chapter 4: The duty to refer cases in England to housing authorities - Homelessness code of guidance for local authorities - Guidance - GOV.UK (www.gov.uk)

[xi] Housing Law and Practice / College of Law Publishing - © The University of Law 2015 - Gail Price LLB (Hons), LLM, Barrister

[xi] Ibid P.158 (2015)

[xii] Possession orders were suspended for a period of time during the Covid pandemic

[xiii] The end of 'no fault' section 21 evictions - House of Commons Library (parliament.uk)

[xiv] Pre-Action Protocol for Possession Claims based on Mortgage or Home Purchase Plan Arrears in Respect of Residential Property

[xv] Loans regulated by the Consumer Credit Act are:

- loans with an amount of credit up to £15,000 taken out before 1 May 1998
- loans with an amount of credit up to £25,000 taken out on or after 1 May 1998
- loans for any sum taken out on or after 6 April 2008

https://england.shelter.org.uk

[xvi] ibid P.167-P.168 (2015)

[xvii] Defending Possession Proceedings / © The Legal Action Group 2022 – HHJ Jan Luba QC/KC, Ann Bevington, John Gallagher, Sam Madge-Wylde and Sarah Steinhardt – 9th ed. P.821-P.822